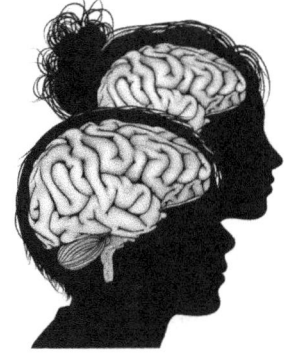

Cranium Crackers

Ignite Your Neurons

Fairy Tales
The Aftermath

Enter the Imaginarium

Created by Julieann Wallace © 2019

Cranium Crackers

I am a teacher (thirty years plus) and love every moment of it. I love the challenges, the successes, and the feeling when I help a child, when I have helped them to succeed in life, to dare to dream and achieve, to feel happy about themselves.

Throughout my teaching career, I always had a wide variety of students in my classes - academically, socially, mentally, physically and behaviourally. And on top of this, I often taught composite classes (two year levels at the same time). I discovered early on in teaching that you need to keep students engaged to stop behaviour issues, especially after they have finished a set task. I also discovered that:
• students like to be challenged
• they like to have open answer type of questions, where there is no right or wrong
• they also like making things with materials instead of just read and write type stuff
• they like to be able to choose which activity they want to do, instead of being told by the teacher
• students like to feel like they have achieved something

So, for the students in my classes, I designed and created "Cranium Crackers".
They were and still are the #1 go-to as a reward for completion of their set work. The activities were sort-after with enthusiasm. I designed the activities to encourage deep thinking and creativity in a fun way and to look at themes and topics from a different point of view.

If you are working with a child or student with the activities, encourage brainstorming for ideas to ignite the neurons! The open ended activities can be completed with guidance or independently. There are no wrong answers, taking away anxiety for children or students who grapple with it.

Enjoy Fairy Tales - The Aftermath!
Julieann Wallace

(Diploma of Teaching, Bachelor of Education, Senior Experienced Teacher,
National Excellence in Teaching Award Nominee x2, Bestselling Author, Illustrator)
www.julieannwallaceauthor.com
https://www.facebook.com/julieannwallace.author/
Instagram: julieannwallace.author
Images: 123rf and Pixabay

Julieann Wallace is a bestselling author, artist and teacher. She writes picture books as Julieann Wallace, and novels as Amelia Grace. She is continually inspired by the gift of imagination, the power of words and the creative arts. She is a self-confessed tea ninja, Cadbury chocoholic, and has a passion for music and art, and tries not to scare her cat, Claude Monet, with her terrible cello playing.

Fairy Tales - The Aftermath © Julieann Wallace 2019
Published by Jacaranda Bloom Books, 2020
ISBN: 978-0-6484244-2-0 (print book)

Cover images: 123rf
Cover design: Lilly Pilly Publishing
Typeset and Format: Lilly Pilly Publishing
lillypillypublishing@outlook.com
www.lillypillypublishing.com

All rights reserved. This book or parts thereof may not be reproduced in any form, stored in any retrieval system, or transmitted in any form by any means—electronic, mechanical, photocopy, recording, or otherwise under copyright law.

Visit *www.julieannwallaceauthor.com* for more **Cranium Cracker** books to ignite imaginations.

Cranium Crackers

Fairy Tales
The Aftermath

Name: _____

Fairy Tale Checklist

As you complete the activities, colour the box

Name:	Recipe For a Fairy Tale
One Hundred Years Later …	Mega Word Search
Lego, Play Dough or Blocks Creation	Write Your Own Fairy Tale
The Wicked Fairy Was Truly Sorry	Fairy Tale Story Map
And Endless Supply of Golden Eggs	Acrostic Poem
Cinderella's Wish List	Help Wanted
Shopping List For the Royal Ball	Castle Mini Project
Wanted Poster	Fee Fi Fo Fum!
Write a Note to the Three Bears	Draw a Map of a Fairy Tale Kingdom
When The 3 Billy Goats Gruff Met the Giant	Fairy Tale Character Profile
Cinderella Visits the Three Bears	Gingerbread People
Design & Build a House of Sticks	Castle Architect
Compose a Song About A Giant	Choose One …
The Answer is 'At Midnight!'	Hero or Heroine
Giant Size Prediction	Little Red Riding Hood's Map
Improve a Witch's Broomstick	Castle Collection
The Magic Finger	Rapunzel's Tower Escape
Create Your Own Fairy Tale Word Search	The Prince is on a Mission
Rumpelstiltskin's New Names	Your Own Fairy Tale Activity
Castle Dungeons & Tunnels	The Dragon Who Lost His Fire
Design a Castle Shield	Ten Fairy Tales That You Never Knew Existed
If You Could Be Any Fairy Tale Character …	Rate The Fairy Tales
Create Your Own Fairy Tale Board Game	A Castle or a Tree?
Design a Crown	Draw a Fairy Tale Scene

One Hundred Years Later ...
List 10 things that will be different in 100 years time

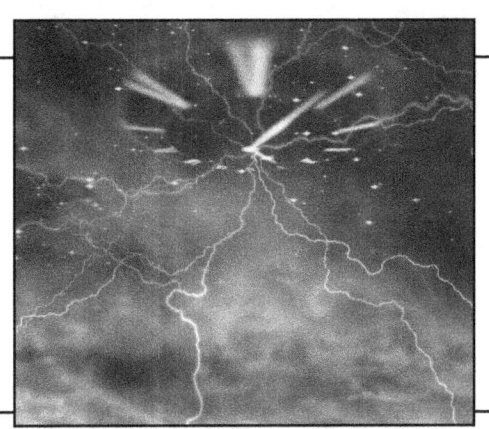

Use Lego, Blocks Or Play Dough
To Create Anything From A Fairy Tale
Photograph it and glue it here, or draw it!

Fairy Tales - The Aftermath

The Wicked Fairy Was Truly Sorry, So She ...

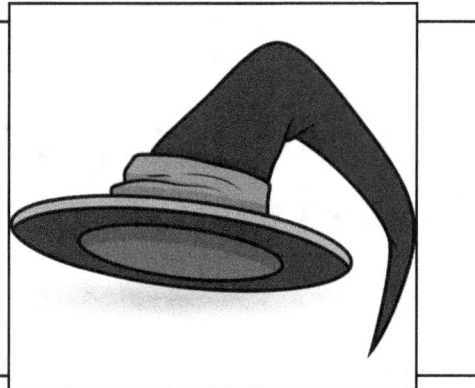

An Endless Supply Of Golden Eggs Might Mean ...

Create Your Own Fairy Tale Word Search for Someone Else to Complete

Words To Find

Write A Shopping List For The Royal Ball
(1000 Guests)

Royal Shopping List For 1000 Guests

Make A WANTED Poster For Any Of The Characters From A Fairy Tale

WANTED!

Name: _____
Description: _____
_____
_____
_____

Crime: _____
_____
_____
_____
_____
_____
_____
_____
_____

REWARD: $

Cinderella's Life Was Not Much Fun!

Write a wish list for her

Write A Note To The Three Bears

Design A Castle Shield

Include These Four Elements On The Shield:

* First Letter Of Surname
* Favourite Food
* Favourite Animal
* Best Weapon

Design & Build A House Of Sticks

List the directions and materials needed to build a house of sticks. Use craft sticks or sticks from trees.

Design your house here. Make sure you label the parts and list the materials that you need. Now build it!

Write A Song About Giants

to the tune of a well known song.
Compose your own music for an extra challenge!

Fairy Tales - The Aftermath

The Answer Is 'At Midnight!'

Make up ten questions to fit the answer.

When The Three Billy Goats Gruff Met A Giant

Rumpelstiltskin Was A Very Unusual Name!

Create ten new names for him and write them with fancy letters.

You May CHOOSE One Of The Following:

- A pair of wings that will take you anywhere you want to go.
- A golden coin that will buy anything you want.
- A goose that lays golden eggs.
- A magic harp that plays such glorious music it makes even the gloomiest person feel happy.
- A magic wand that heals injuries and illnesses.
- A pair of shoes that enables you to win any race.
- A magic lamp with just three wishes.
- Prayer

**Choose carefully –
Write reasons 'for' and 'against' your choice.
Give reasons for your decisions.**

I Choose:

Reasons for:

Reasons against:

Cinderella Went To Visit The Three Bears

What Happened?

Fairy Tales - The Aftermath

The Prince Or Princess Is On A Mission

What might that be?
Write about it (story or cartoon)
or draw the mission.

Design Secret Underground Passageways And Dungeons
for a Castle

Improve A Witch's Broomstick

So that it is faster and more fun to ride

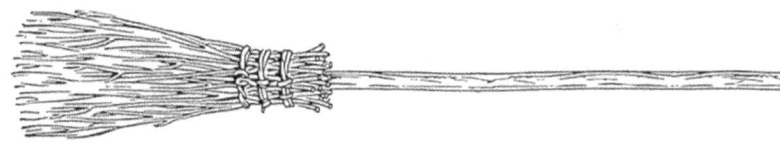

Design A Crown
for a King, Queen, Prince or Princess

Draw A Map
Of The FairyTale Kingdom

Fairy Tale Mega Word Search
Can you find them all?

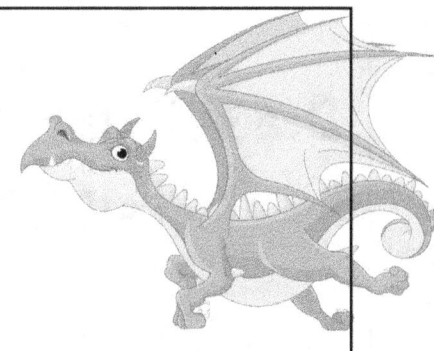

G	F	D	R	A	G	O	N	A	P	R	I	N	C	E	S	S	B	E	S
I	O	I	F	O	R	E	S	T	Q	T	R	E	E	S	O	G	R	E	T
N	X	A	U	T	H	O	R	I	U	A	W	O	L	F	H	E	R	O	E
G	B	E	A	S	T	A	X	E	E	D	W	A	R	F	R	N	M	J	P
E	B	I	S	P	E	L	L	A	E	F	A	I	R	Y	U	I	A	A	M
R	E	G	O	E	L	V	E	S	N	G	I	A	N	T	N	G	G	C	O
B	A	C	E	N	T	U	R	Y	F	A	N	T	A	S	Y	H	I	K	T
R	R	F	A	T	H	E	R	J	O	U	R	N	E	Y	A	T	C	I	H
E	S	Q	U	E	S	T	I	R	O	Y	A	L	A	N	I	M	A	L	E
A	F	A	I	R	Y	T	A	L	E	H	A	P	P	I	L	Y	M	E	R
D	H	E	R	O	I	N	E	C	H	A	R	A	C	T	E	R	F	O	X
A	C	I	N	D	E	R	E	L	L	A	I	M	O	N	S	T	E	R	C
E	N	C	H	A	N	T	E	D	G	R	A	P	U	N	Z	E	L	S	O
A	N	C	I	E	N	T	B	O	O	K	P	A	F	T	E	R	W	H	Y
C	T	M	O	T	H	E	R	S	E	E	S	N	O	W	W	H	I	T	E
H	P	R	I	N	C	E	W	T	R	O	L	L	X	W	I	C	K	E	D
I	Z	P	I	G	S	L	G	O	D	M	O	T	H	E	R	T	A	L	E
L	R	I	D	D	L	E	O	W	I	S	E	W	I	Z	A	R	D	N	O
D	D	G	O	L	D	I	L	O	C	K	S	C	M	Y	T	H	Y	A	Y
C	A	S	T	L	E	R	W	O	O	D	S	E	V	E	R	K	I	N	G

DRAGON	CASTLE	PRINCE	PRINCESS	KING
QUEEN	CINDERELLA	RAPUNZEL	OGRE	JACK
GINGERBREAD	BEAST	GOLDILOCKS	WOLF	PIGS
BEARS	SNOW WHITE	FOREST	SPELL	TREES
ANCIENT	BOOK	CENTURY	CHILD	AUTHOR
DWARF	ELVES	ENCHANTED	WOODS	FAIRY
FAIRYTALE	FANTASY	FOX	GIANT	GODMOTHER
FATHER	MOTHER	STEPMOTHER	HAPPILY	EVER
AFTER	HERO	HEROINE	JOURNEY	TROLL
MYTH	QUEST	RIDDLE	TALE	ROYAL
WICKED	WISE	WIZARD	CHARACTER	MAGIC
ANIMAL	RUN	MONSTER	FOX	NIGHT

List Ten Fairy Tales That You Didn't Know Existed

	Title	Author
1		
2		
3		
4		
5		
6		
7		
8		
9		
10		

Draw a character from one of the titles

© Julieann Wallace

Write Your Fairy Tale
You are now the author, and anything is possible.

Your story must contain the following characters:
- hero/heroine
- villain
- animals

Plus, you can have other characters as well.

Your story needs:
- An introduction
- A complication – What is the problem?
  What happens, who is involved?
  How are the characters feeling now?
- And a solution – How is the problem solved?
  What emotions are felt?

Make your story better with:
- including the five senses - sight, touch, smell, taste, hearing
- interesting sentence beginnings
- talking between characters
- descriptions
- adjectives (describing words)
- verbs (action words)

and don't forget paragraphs!

Story Plan

Some authors use a plan to write down story ideas before they write. Some authors don't use a plan, their ideas come to them as they write.

Here is a story plan to use if you like to plan before you write. And remember, your story plan can change – especially if you come up with a better idea!

Narrative Plan

Title

Setting
Who ? _____
When ? _____
Where ? _____

Complication (problem)
What Happens? _____

Why? _____

Resolution
How is the problem solved? How does it end?

Writing Checklist ...

Have you • re-read your story to make sure that it makes sense?	Have you added: • describing words • what the characters see, hear, smell, taste, feel • emotions • action • speech	Have you checked punctuation: • fullstops (.) • commas (,) • talking marks ("Hello," I said.) • exclamation marks (!) • circled spelling you are not (shure) about	Have you got capital letters for: • the title • the beginning of sentences • the names of characters • the names of places

© Julieann Wallace

Read A Fairy Tale & Complete the Story Map

Title:

Author:

Characters

Setting

Resolution

Problem

Action:

Fairy Tales - The Aftermath

Acrostic Poem

F _____
A _____
I _____
R _____
Y _____
T _____
A _____
L _____
E _____
S _____

Help Wanted!

Which fairy tale character needs help, and why? Use persuasive words!

HELP!
Help Me! Help Me, Please!

_____
_____
_____
_____
_____
_____
_____
_____
_____
_____
_____
_____
_____
_____
_____
_____

Signed: _____

Castle Mini Project

What is a castle?

Where were they built?

Why were they built?

Common features of castles:

Castle Architect

Design your own castle.
Choose either to show it from the exterior,
or the interior with a floor plan.

CASTLE COLLECTION

Find or draw pictures of casltes or parts of castles and make a collage out of them.

Fairy Tale Scene
Draw a scene from any fairy tale

Fairy Tale Character Profile

Who?

Which fairy tale?

Strengths

Weaknesses

If you could change one thing about the character, what would it be?

The Dragon Has Lost His Fire

List five ideas about how the dragon could get its flame going again.

Just Suppose You Had A 'Magic Finger' ...

What are all the things that might happen?

Predict What Would Happen If Everyone Became Giant—Sized?

Would you rather be ...

a castle or a tree?
Why?

Draw a Map For Little Red Riding Hood

so she doesn't get lost
going to her grandmother's house.

Fairy Tales - The Aftermath

CREATE Your Own Fairy Tale Board Game
Make rules and game cards to go with it.
Now play it.

If You Could Choose To Be Any Fairy Tale Character
— what would you be, and why?

Draw yourself as the fairy tale character

Rate the Fairy Tales

Title	My Opinion
Cinderella	☹ 🙂 😎
Beauty and the Beast	☹ 🙂 😎
Jack and the Beanstalk	☹ 🙂 😎
Rapunzel	☹ 🙂 😎
Rumpelstiltskin	☹ 🙂 😎
Sleeping Beauty	☹ 🙂 😎
Snow White and the Seven Dwarfs	☹ 🙂 😎
Goldilocks and the Three Bears	☹ 🙂 😎
Little Red Riding Hood	☹ 🙂 😎
The Frog Prince	☹ 🙂 😎

Do you like Fairy Tales?
Explain your answer

_____
_____
_____
_____
_____
_____
_____
_____

© Julieann Wallace

Rapunzel's Tower Escape
Rapunzel is trapped in a tower.
Design an escape for her.

Gingerbread People

Dress the gingerbread people.
You can only use four colors,
and no gingerbread people can be
identical. Add accessories if you like.

Recipe for a Fairy Tale
What writing ingredients make the best fairy tales?

Fairy Tales - The Aftermath

Choose to be a Hero/Heroine
Who are you, and who or what will you rescue, and why?

Fee Fi Fo Fum!
I Smell a Sandwich!
Create a giant sandwich
for a hungry giant.

Create Your Own Fairy Tale Activity

The Prince Needs Rescuing

Where is he? Who rescues him? How is he rescued?

You Find a Dragon
and want to keep it as a pet.
What do you do?

The Imaginarium.
Draw. Write. Create. Design.

The Imaginarium.
Draw. Write. Create. Design.

The Imaginarium.
Draw. Write. Create. Design.

www.ingramcontent.com/pod-product-compliance
Lightning Source LLC
Chambersburg PA
CBHW080856010526
44107CB00057B/2590